Jane Lawrie

simplyeggs

foreword by Antony Worrall Thompson

SIMON & SCHUSTER

A VIACOM COMPANY

First published in Great Britain by Simon & Schuster UK Ltd, 2001
A Viacom Company

ISBN 0 74320 732 7

1 3 5 7 9 10 8 6 4 2

Simon & Schuster UK Ltd
Africa House
64-78 Kingsway
London WC2B 6AH

Design: Blue Banana
Photographs: Joff Lee
Typesetting: Stylize Digital Artwork
Printed and bound in Hong Kong

Contents

FOREWORD
by Antony Worrall Thompson

I'm thrilled to see that the marvellous egg, nature's original fast food, has a book completely devoted to it.

I must confess that I'm a real fan of eggs; their versatility and ease of cooking makes them ideal for busy people. A hectic lifestyle often dictates what types of food you have time to eat and people today have different priorities from when I first started cooking. Sadly, home cooking often comes a long way down the list. However, with a food like eggs, there's no excuse. They're delicious, nutritious, and incredibly quick to cook.

I have to admit I've tried just about every method of cooking eggs; I suppose I'm a bit of a connoisseur, but even I'm really impressed with the variety of tempting recipes in this new book. I'm sure that these recipes will inspire even the most unimaginative or inexperienced cook. And there's no reason why anyone should be nervous about cooking eggs. They really are very easy; whichever way you prefer them. My favourite eggs are poached eggs.

I also think that it's really nice to be able to know that the products you're using are of the highest quality. Eggs have had a bit of stick in the past, but now with the return of the Lion Quality mark you can be sure that the egg you're eating really is among the best and safest in the world. Lion Quality eggs come from British hens vaccinated against salmonella and there's even a 'best before' date on the egg shell to tell you how fresh they are. In fact, egg production is one area of British agriculture that is a real success story.

There's good news on the health front as well. The latest scientific research shows that most people can eat an egg a day without worrying about raising their blood cholesterol levels.

I hope you enjoy the book as much as I have.

Introduction

Eggs have symbolised many things throughout the ages. In past times they have represented mystery, magic and medicine and have been displayed embellished with jewels, painted in fine colours or dyed.

Today when we think of eggs we generally think of a food commodity. What we should appreciate is that the egg is an incredibly diverse ingredient; it represents one of the most nutritionally complete, naturally produced foods that money can buy. Indeed, the humble egg provides many of the essential nutrients that make up a balanced diet. So, however you choose to have yours, the egg has a great deal to offer.

Nutrition: the all-round *Good Egg*

Calories

Eggs are relatively low in calories. A medium egg provides around 76 Kcal (318 Kilojoules), meaning that one egg per day contributes only 3% of the total calorie needs of an adult. So not only are eggs ideal as an everyday food for most of the population, they are also ideal for those wanting to reduce their weight.

Protein

A regular supply of protein in the diet is essential for the maintenance, repair and growth of body tissues. This is particularly important in childhood, adolescence and pregnancy when rate of growth is at its highest.

Eggs are considered to contain one of the finest quality proteins and thus are the benchmark by which all other proteins are judged. Protein, including all eight essential amino acids, makes up half of the weight of an egg. A medium egg contributes about 12% of a man's daily protein needs and 14% of a woman's. Eggs are a good source of protein for everyone, in particular for those avoiding meat and fish.

Cholesterol

Cholesterol is a waxy, fat-like substance that is essential in the human body. There are two basic types of cholesterol: blood cholesterol and dietary cholesterol. Blood cholesterol is the level of cholesterol circulating in your blood stream and dietary cholesterol is the cholesterol that appears naturally in many animal-based foods, including eggs, meat and shellfish.

When too much cholesterol appears in the blood stream it can lead to heart disease. Because of the relatively high cholesterol content of eggs, some people have had reservations about eating eggs in the past. However, the latest scientific research shows that our blood cholesterol levels are elevated by the saturated fat we eat, rather than the dietary cholesterol.

This means that most people eating a diet low in saturated fat can eat an egg a day without worrying about raising their blood cholesterol levels.

Fat

We mainly eat three different types of fat: saturated fat (SFA), monounsaturated fat (MUFA) and polyunsaturated fat (PUFA). Fat is essential in our diet for many reasons, but most people tend to eat too much leading to a variety of complaints including obesity, heart disease and mobility problems. The consensus of medical opinion is that we should cut down on fat, in particular on saturated fat. Eggs are relatively low in saturated fat; a medium egg contains only 1.6 g. This makes eggs an ideal part of a healthy diet that's low in saturated fat.

Vitamins and minerals

Eggs contain a wealth of vitamins. In particular they are an excellent source of the B vitamin group which performs many vital functions. Eggs also provide vitamin A – essential for normal growth and development – and a useful amount of vitamin E – a powerful antioxidant that gives protection against heart disease and some cancers. Vitamin D is also present; it promotes proper mineral absorption and good bone health.

Eggs are a good source of minerals, particularly iodine, required in making thyroid hormones, and phosphorus, essential for healthy bones and teeth, and many of the essential trace elements including zinc for improved immunity, iron for red blood cell formation and selenium, which gives some protection against heart disease.

Lion Quality and Egg Safety

In the past there have been some concerns over the safety of eggs. The Lion Quality mark was relaunched by the UK egg industry in 1998 to give shoppers confidence when buying and eating eggs. Today Lion Quality eggs are among the safest in the world.

All Lion Quality eggs come from hens that have been vaccinated against salmonella and are fully traceable through a certification scheme. Along with the Lion Quality mark, a 'best before' date also appears on the egg box and egg shell. This guarantees that the eggs are even fresher than required by law.

The Lion Quality standard is set by the British Egg Industry Council under the Lion Code of Practice and is vigorously monitored by independent auditors.

When handling eggs it's important to remember to store them in the refrigerator to ensure maximum freshness.

Production Methods

There are three main laying systems in the UK. The most common is the laying cage system which represents around 76% of eggs produced. Hens are kept inside cages with up to five birds to a cage. The barn system contributes around 6% of total egg production. The hens wander around freely inside houses which provide litter and perches. Free-range eggs represent around 18% of total UK egg production. Hens are kept in similar conditions to barn hens, but with continuous access to outdoor runs and natural vegetation during the daytime.

Cooking eggs

Begin with Boiling

Boiling an egg is simple once you have mastered the basics. To prevent eggs cracking, make a small pin prick in the shell at the rounded end to allow the steam to escape.

Place 2 large Lion Quality eggs in a small pan. Cover with at least 2.5 cm (1 inch) of cold water, add a pinch of salt and place the pan on a high heat.

When the water is almost boiling, gently stir the eggs and set a kitchen timer for one of the timings below. Reduce heat slightly to keep water bubbling but not fast boiling and stir the eggs once more.

Cooking time in minutes	Results
3	**really soft boiled yolk and set white**
4	**slightly set yolk and set white**
5	**firmer yolk and white**
6	**hard boiled with lightly soft yolk**
7	**firmly hard boiled**

Once cooking time is complete, remove the eggs from the pan with slotted spoon and serve immediately with hot buttered toast soldiers.

Freshly Fried

A symbol of the great British breakfast, fried eggs are a real family favourite.

Put 3 tablespoons of vegetable oil or 25 g (1 oz) of butter and 1 tablespoon of vegetable oil in a small frying pan and place over a medium heat. When the fat is hot, use a knife to crack the shell of a large Lion Quality egg. Tip the egg straight into the frying pan.

Cook over a medium heat for 1–2 minutes or until the white is set. Tilt the pan slightly and use a teaspoon to scoop the hot fat over the egg until the yolk is cooked to your liking.

For over easy eggs, carefully slide a spatula underneath the cooked egg and flip over to cook the yolk for 1 minute. Once cooked, lift the egg out using a spatula and place on kitchen paper to drain the excess fat. Serve with a slice of buttered toast or rashers of grilled bacon and tomatoes.

To prevent the egg sticking to the pan during frying, sprinkle a little salt on the hot butter or oil before adding the egg to the pan.

The Original Omelette

This is the classic recipe for a folded or French-style omelette; it's quick and easy, producing a meal in minutes.

Gently beat 3 large Lion Quality eggs together with salt, pepper and a teaspoon of cold water. Melt 25 g (1 oz) butter in a medium frying pan over a high heat. When the butter is bubbling, pour the egg mixture into the centre of the pan.

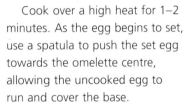

Cook over a high heat for 1–2 minutes. As the egg begins to set, use a spatula to push the set egg towards the omelette centre, allowing the uncooked egg to run and cover the base.

Continue until no runny egg remains. Cook the set omelette for another minute, then loosen the edges with a spatula and fold the omelette in half. Tilt the pan and slide the omelette onto a warm plate. Serve immediately on its own or with a crisp green salad.

Perfectly Poached

Poached eggs are so simple to make and, cooked without any fat, they are really healthy too.

Fill a large frying pan with 5 cm (2 inches) of water. Add a pinch of salt and a dash of vinegar to help set the egg. Bring the water to a gentle boil. Crack a large Lion Quality egg into a small bowl and then tip it into the simmering water. Reduce the heat so the water gently bubbles around the eggs.

Set a kitchen timer for one of the timings below.

Cooking time in minutes	Results
3	completely runny yolk
4	slightly set yolk with a runny middle
5	firm yolk

When the cooking time is complete, carefully remove the poached egg from the boiling water using a slotted spoon.

Place on kitchen paper to drain. Serve immediately on a warmed, buttered muffin or slice of buttered toast.

Superbly Scrambled

Scrambled eggs are one of the quickest and most convenient ways of cooking eggs.

Gently beat 2 large Lion Quality eggs together with a pinch of salt and pepper. For a softer result add 2 tablespoons of milk to the eggs. Melt a knob of butter in a non-stick pan over a medium heat. When sizzling, add the egg mixture.

Stir with a wooden spoon. Continue to stir the eggs for 1–2 minutes, scraping the egg off the base of the pan as it sets.

When most of the egg has set, remove the pan from the heat and continue to stir for 30 seconds until fully scrambled. Serve immediately with a round of buttered toast.

Egg custard

Preparation and cooking time: 10 minutes
Serves 4

300 ml (½ pint) milk
300 ml (½ pint) single cream
4 large Lion Quality egg yolks
4 tablespoons caster sugar
½ teaspoon vanilla essence

1 Put the milk and cream in medium heavy-based pan and slowly bring to the boil. In a large bowl, beat the egg yolks, sugar and vanilla together until creamy.
2 Pour the hot milk and cream on to the egg yolks and stir well. Rinse out the saucepan. Strain through a nylon sieve back into the saucepan.
3 Place the pan on the lowest heat and cook, stirring constantly, until the custard thickens enough to coat the back of a spoon and has the consistency of single cream. Pour into a warm jug and serve with hot puddings.

Sabayon Sauce

Preparation and cooking time: 10 minutes
Serves 4

4 large Lion Quality egg yolks
4 tablespoons caster sugar
2 tablespoons sherry or sweet white wine

1 Put the egg yolks and sugar together in a heatproof bowl and place over a pan of simmering water. Use an electric whisk to whisk the mixture until thick and frothy. The mixture should be thick enough to leave a ribbon trail on the surface when the whisks are lifted.
2 Remove from the heat, add the sherry or wine and whisk until cooled slightly. Serve spooned over fruity puddings.

sauces

Eggs form the basis of some really classic sauces – here are four favourites.

Hollandaise Sauce

Preparation and cooking time: 5 minutes
Serves 4

75 g (2¾ oz) butter
2 teaspoons Dijon mustard
2 tablespoons white wine vinegar
2 large Lion Quality egg yolks
salt and freshly ground black pepper

1 Melt the butter and set aside to cool slightly. Place the mustard, vinegar, egg yolks and seasoning in a heatproof bowl and place over a pan of simmering water.
2 Whisking constantly with a balloon whisk, gradually add the melted butter until the sauce is smooth and thick. Remove from the heat and thin as required with 1–2 tablespoons of warm water. Serve warm.

Salad cream dressing

Preparation and cooking time: 10 minutes
Serves 4

1 large Lion Quality egg
6 tablespoons olive oil
juice of ½ lemon
½ teaspoon caster sugar
½ teaspoon Dijon mustard

1 Put the egg in a small pan, cover with cold water and bring to the boil. Boil for 6 minutes. Drain, rinse in cold water tapping the shells all over. When cold, peel away the shell.
2 Place the egg and remaining ingredients in a food processor and whizz together until a smooth dressing forms. Season to taste. Chill until required.

Big Brekky Baked Eggs

Preparation time: 10 minutes + 20–25 minutes cooking
Serves 4

25 g (1 oz) butter
175 g (6 oz) button mushrooms, sliced
1 green pepper, de-seeded and diced
225 g (8 oz) Frankfurter sausages, sliced
175 g (6 oz) cherry tomatoes, halved
4 large Lion Quality eggs
4 tablespoons single cream
salt and freshly ground black pepper
hot buttered toast, to serve

1 Preheat the oven to Gas Mark 4/180°C/350°F. Melt the butter in a medium pan and add the mushrooms and pepper. Sauté for 3–4 minutes or until soft. Stir in the Frankfurters and cherry tomatoes. Remove from the heat and season to taste.
2 Divide the mixture between four oiled shallow ovenproof dishes and make a well in the centre of each. Carefully crack an egg into each well. Place the dishes on a baking tray and pour the cream over the egg yolks. Cover the tray with foil and bake for 20–25 minutes or until the eggs are set. Serve with hot buttered toast.

Breakfast Sizzle

Preparation and cooking time: 20 minutes
Serves 4

3 tablespoons vegetable oil
450 g (1 lb) cooked new potatoes, sliced
4 rashers back bacon, de-rinded and sliced
100 g (3½ oz) mushrooms, sliced
175 g (6 oz) cherry tomatoes, halved
4 large Lion Quality eggs
salt and freshly ground black pepper

1 Heat 1 tablespoon of the oil in a large non-stick frying pan. Add the potatoes and cook for 4 minutes, stirring occasionally. Add the bacon and mushrooms and cook over a high heat for 4–5 minutes or until golden. Stir in the tomatoes and cook for another minute. Season and transfer to a dish. Keep warm.
2 Wipe out the pan and add the remaining oil. When hot, carefully crack the eggs into the pan. Fry over a medium heat until cooked to your liking (page 6).
3 To serve, divide the potato and bacon mixture between four warm plates and top each with a fried egg. Serve immediately.

breakfast

If breakfast is the most important meal of the day, then eggs must be the perfect breakfast food. They're quick to prepare, excellent nutritionally and lend themselves to all sorts of tempting dishes.

Buck Rarebit

Preparation and cooking time: 20 minutes
Serves 2

150 ml (¼ pint) milk
1 tablespoon plain flour
1 teaspoon mustard powder
25 g (1 oz) butter
50 g (1¾ oz) Cheddar, grated
a dash of vinegar
400 g can baked beans
2 large Lion Quality eggs
2 slices wholemeal bread
salt and freshly ground black pepper

1 Place the milk, flour, mustard and butter in a medium pan. Whisk together with a balloon whisk and slowly bring to the boil, whisking until the mixture boils and thickens. Simmer for 1 minute. Stir in half the cheese and season to taste. Set aside.
2 Fill a large frying pan with salted water, add the vinegar and bring to the boil.
3 Meanwhile put the beans in a pan and gently heat for 2–3 minutes or until piping hot.
4 Poach the eggs in the simmering water for 3–5 minutes until cooked to your liking (page 7).
5 Meanwhile toast the bread on both sides under a hot grill. Arrange the toast on two heatproof serving plates. Top with the baked beans and place a poached egg on top of each. Spoon over the cheese sauce and sprinkle over the remaining cheese. Place each plate under the grill and cook for 1 minute until golden.

Sautéed Mushrooms with Poached Eggs

Preparation and cooking time: 20 minutes
Serves 4

a dash of vinegar
1 tablespoon vegetable oil
a bunch of spring onions, trimmed and sliced
1 garlic clove, chopped
225 g (8 oz) mixed mushrooms (e.g. flat, chestnut, oyster, shiitake), wiped and sliced if large
2 tablespoons crème fraîche
4 large Lion Quality eggs
4 slices brioche or bread
salt and freshly ground black pepper

1 Fill a large frying pan with salted water, add the vinegar and bring to the boil.
2 Heat the oil in a non-stick frying pan and add the onions, garlic and mushrooms. Sauté over a high heat for 5 minutes or until the mushrooms are tender.
3 Remove from the heat, stir in the crème fraîche and then season to taste with salt and pepper. Keep warm.
4 Poach the eggs in the simmering water for 3–5 minutes until cooked to your liking (page 7).
5 Meanwhile, toast the brioche or bread on both sides under a hot grill. To serve, put the toast on four warm plates, spoon over the mushroom mixture and top with the poached egg. Sprinkle with black pepper and serve immediately.

Smoked Salmon and Coddled Egg Muffins

Preparation and cooking time: 15 minutes
Serves 4

6 large Lion Quality eggs
2 tablespoons snipped fresh dill
1 tablespoon crème fraîche
4 muffins, split
4 slices smoked salmon
salt and freshly ground black pepper

1 Put the eggs in a medium pan, cover with cold water and bring to the boil. Set the timer and cook for 5 minutes. Drain, run under cold water until cool enough to handle and then carefully peel away the shells.
2 Put the eggs in a bowl and chop them roughly with a knife and fork. Add the dill and crème fraîche and season with salt and pepper to taste.
3 Toast the muffins under a hot grill, turning once, until golden on both sides. Top the muffins with smoked salmon and spoon the egg mixture over. Serve immediately.

Eggs Benedict

Preparation and cooking time: 15 minutes
Serves 4

100 g (3½ oz) butter
2 teaspoons wholegrain mustard
4 teaspoons white wine vinegar
2 large Lion Quality egg yolks
4 large Lion Quality eggs
4 white muffins
8 thin slices smoked ham
salt and freshly ground black pepper
parsley, to garnish

1 For the sauce melt 75 g (2¾ oz) of the butter. Put the mustard, half the vinegar, the egg yolks and seasoning in a heatproof bowl over a pan of simmering water. Gradually whisk in the butter until the sauce is smooth and thick. Remove from the heat and whisk in 1 tablespoon of hot water to thin the sauce slightly. Keep warm.
2 Fill a large frying pan with salted water, add the remaining vinegar and bring to the boil. Poach the eggs in simmering water until cooked to your liking (page 7).
3 Meanwhile, split and lightly toast the muffins and spread with the remaining butter. Place the muffins on four serving plates. Top with slices of ham and a poached egg, and pour over the sauce. Grind over some pepper and serve garnished with parsley.

brunch

On a lazy morning, gather together friends and family and indulge in a feast of flavours with one of these stylish brunch ideas.

Ranch Style Eggs

Preparation and cooking time: 20 minutes
Serves 4

3 tablespoons vegetable oil
1 red onion, sliced
1 green pepper, de-seeded and sliced
1 red pepper, de-seeded and sliced
1 garlic clove, crushed
1–2 red chillies, de-seeded and diced
8 large Lion Quality eggs
2 teaspoons ground cumin
2 teaspoons ground paprika
3 tablespoons chopped fresh coriander
4 flour tortillas
salt and freshly ground black pepper
crisp grilled bacon, to serve

1 Heat the oil in a large pan, add the onion and peppers and sauté for 5 minutes or until soft. Add the garlic and chillies and cook for 1 minute.
2 Beat the eggs together with the spices and seasoning.
3 Pour the eggs into the pan, and cook over a gentle heat for 3–4 minutes, stirring to softly scramble the eggs. Remove from the heat and stir in the coriander.
4 Meanwhile warm the tortillas according to the instructions on the packet. Divide the eggs between the tortillas and serve warm with crisp grilled bacon.

Caerphilly, Leek and Bacon Welsh Cakes

Preparation time: 10 minutes + 15–20 minutes cooking
Serves 4

oil for frying
75 g (2¾ oz) streaky bacon, chopped
1 leek, chopped
225 g (8 oz) plain flour
1 teaspoon baking powder
a pinch of salt
50 g (1¾ oz) butter
50 g (1¾ oz) Caerphilly cheese, crumbled
6 large Lion Quality eggs
butter

1 Preheat the oven to Gas Mark 4/180°C/350°F. Add a teaspoon of oil to a frying pan, add the bacon and cook for 3–4 minutes or until pale golden. Add the leek and cook for a further 2 minutes. Allow to cool. Sift the flour, baking powder and salt into a large bowl and rub in the butter. Stir in the cheese and cooled bacon and leeks.
2 Beat 2 eggs and stir enough egg into the flour mixture to make a soft dough. Lightly knead and cut in half. Roll each half out into a 13 cm (5-inch) circle and cut into quarters.
3 Place a griddle or heavy frying pan over a medium low heat. Add the Welsh cakes to the pan in batches of 4. Cook for 4–5 minutes or until the base is golden. Turn over and cook for a further 3–4 minutes. Place on a baking sheet. Bake for 5 minutes while you prepare the eggs.
4 Heat 2 tablespoons oil in a non-stick frying pan, crack in the remaining eggs and fry over a medium heat until cooked to your liking (page 6). Split the warm Welsh cakes in half, spread with a little butter and top with a fried egg.

Fried Egg and Ham Sandwich

Preparation and cooking time: 10 minutes
Serves 1

2 thin slices bread
2 tablespoons tomato ketchup
2 slices wafer-thin ham
3 tablespoons vegetable oil
1 large Lion Quality egg
15 g (½ oz) Cheddar cheese, grated
chopped parsley, to garnish

1 Spread one slice of bread with tomato ketchup and top with the ham. Sandwich together with the second slice of bread. Use a 7.5 cm (3-inch) round cutter to press out a circle from the centre of the ham sandwich (eat while you cook the egg!).
2 Heat 2 tablespoons of oil in a non-stick frying pan, add the sandwich and fry for 2 minutes or until golden-brown on the base. Turn over, add the remaining oil and carefully crack the egg into the hole. Cook over a low heat for 2 minutes or until the egg is beginning to set.
3 Sprinkle over the cheese then pop the pan under a hot grill and cook for 30 seconds to 1 minute or until the egg has set. Transfer to a plate, sprinkle with chopped parsley and add a good dollop of tomato ketchup. Serve immediately with a mug of coffee.

Quick Vegetable and Egg Pizza

Preparation and cooking time: 20 minutes
Serves 2

2 ciabatta rolls, halved
2 tablespoons olive oil
4 mushrooms, sliced
½ green pepper, de-seeded and sliced
2 Lion Quality eggs
2 tablespoons pesto sauce
4 tomatoes, sliced
50 g (1¾ oz) Cheddar, grated

1 Preheat the grill to high. Slice the rolls in half and toast for 1–2 minutes or until golden brown.
2 Heat the oil in a non-stick frying pan. Add the mushrooms and pepper and fry for 2–3 minutes or until soft. Transfer to a plate with a slotted spoon.
3 Carefully crack the eggs into the frying pan and fry until cooked to your liking (page 6).
4 Meanwhile top the ciabatta with pesto sauce, sliced tomatoes and cook under the grill for 2 minutes or until the tomatoes are soft. Top with the mushrooms and peppers. With a spatula place a fried egg on top. Sprinkle over the cheese and grill for 2–3 minutes or until the cheese is golden and bubbling. Serve immediately.

snacks

Eggs are the original convenience food, perfect for filling that hungry hole any time of the day (or night!)

Egg and Bacon Jackets

Preparation time: 20 minutes + 1 hour cooking
Serves 4

4 large baking potatoes
175 g (6 oz) streaky bacon, rind removed
a dash of vinegar
4 large Lion Quality eggs
50 g (1¾ oz) butter
4 tablespoons snipped fresh chives
100 g (3½ oz) cherry tomatoes, halved

1 Preheat the oven to Gas Mark 7/220°C/425°F. Bake the potatoes for about 1 hour or until tender. Alternatively prick the potatoes all over with a fork and microwave on high for 10 minutes or until tender.
2 Meanwhile cook the bacon under a hot grill for 6–8 minutes, turning once, until crisp and golden. Snip into bite-sized pieces and set aside.
3 When the potatoes are cooked, bring a large frying pan of salted water to the boil. Add the vinegar. Poach the eggs in the simmering water for 3–5 minutes until cooked to your liking (page 7).
4 Cut a cross in the top of each potato, open out and scoop out the flesh leaving a 1 cm (½-inch) shell. Mash the scooped-out potato with the butter and stir in the chives, bacon and tomatoes.
5 Heap the mixture back into the skins and place a poached egg on top of each. Serve immediately.

Italian Baked Eggs

Preparation time: 15 minutes + 15 minutes cooking
Serves 4

2 tablespoons olive oil
1 large onion, chopped
2 garlic cloves, chopped
350 g (12 oz) young spinach leaves, washed
15 g packet fresh basil leaves, snipped
½ teaspoon freshly grated nutmeg
4 large Lion Quality eggs
4 tablespoons crème fraîche
25 g (1 oz) freshly grated Parmesan cheese
25 g (1 oz) pine nuts
salt and freshly ground black pepper
crusty bread, to serve

1 Preheat the oven to Gas Mark 5/190°C/375°F. Heat the oil in a large pan, add the onion and cook over a medium heat for 5 minutes or until golden. Add the garlic and then stir in the spinach. Cover the pan and cook for 3 minutes, shaking the pan occasionally, until the leaves are wilted. Transfer to a sieve and squeeze out the excess liquid. Return the spinach to the pan and add the basil and nutmeg. Season to taste with salt and pepper.
2 Divide the spinach between four small ovenproof dishes and make a well in the centre of the mixture. Carefully crack an egg into each dish. Spoon over the crème fraîche and scatter over the cheese and pine nuts. Bake for 10–15 minutes or until the eggs are set. Serve with crusty bread.

Coddled Eggs on Crumpets

Preparation and cooking time: 15 minutes
Serves 4

4 large Lion Quality eggs
4 crumpets
4 tablespoons sun-dried tomato paste
150 g packet mozzarella, sliced
4 tomatoes, sliced

1 Place the eggs in a small pan. Cover with cold water and bring to the boil. Set the timer and cook for 3½ minutes. Drain, run under cold water until cool enough to handle and then carefully peel away the shells.
2 Meanwhile toast the crumpets under a medium grill for 3 minutes on each side. Spread with the tomato paste, top with the mozzarella and tomatoes. Cook under the grill for a further 2 minutes or until the cheese is pale golden. Top with the eggs and serve immediately.

Pitta Pockets

Preparation and cooking time: 15 minutes
Serves 4

4 large Lion Quality eggs
4 tablespoons mayonnaise
1 teaspoon medium curry paste
1 tablespoon mango chutney
4 wholemeal pitta breads
2 tomatoes, sliced
50 g (1¾ oz) herb salad leaves
¼ cucumber, sliced
salt and freshly ground black pepper

1 Put the eggs in a medium pan, cover with cold water and bring to the boil. Boil for 7 minutes and then drain and rinse in cold water, tapping the shells all over. When cold, peel away the shells and put in a bowl.
2 Roughly chop the eggs with a knife and fork and add the mayonnaise, curry paste and chutney. Mix well and season to taste.
3 Place the pitta bread under a hot grill or in a toaster and toast for 1–2 minutes, turning once until they are puffed up and pale golden. Cut each in half, open out the pocket and fill with the egg mixture, tomatoes, salad and cucumber. Serve immediately or wrap and chill for packed lunches. Once filled they are best eaten within 6 hours.

Cheese, Tomato and Ham Soufflé Omelette

Preparation and cooking time: 10 minutes
Serves 1

2 large Lion Quality eggs, separated
1 teaspoon wholegrain mustard
15 g (½ oz) butter
100 g (3½ oz) cherry tomatoes, halved
1 slice cooked ham, cut into strips
25 g (1 oz) mature Cheddar, grated
salt and freshly ground black pepper

1 Beat the egg yolks with the mustard and salt and pepper. Whisk the egg whites in a clean bowl until they form soft peaks. Gently fold the whites into the egg yolks.

2 Preheat the grill to high. Melt the butter in a medium omelette pan and when sizzling pour in the egg mixture. Cook over a medium heat for 1–2 minutes or until the base is golden.

3 Place the omelette under the hot grill and cook for a further 1–2 minutes or until the top is golden. Scatter over the tomatoes, ham and cheese and fold in half. Serve immediately.

Herby Mushroom and Cheese Omelette

Preparation and cooking time: 25 minutes
Serves 4

50 g (1¾ oz) butter
450 g (1 lb) mixed mushrooms, sliced
1 garlic clove, crushed
12 large Lion Quality eggs
4 tablespoons chopped mixed fresh herbs
75 g (2¾ oz) Gruyère cheese, grated
salt and freshly ground black pepper

1 Melt half the butter in a medium omelette pan. Add the mushrooms and garlic and sauté for 3 minutes or until soft. Season well and transfer to a dish and keep warm.

2 Beat the eggs together with the herbs and seasoning. Melt a quarter of the remaining butter in the frying pan until bubbling. Add a quarter of the egg mixture and cook for 3–4 minutes to make an omelette (page 7).

3 Scatter a quarter of the mushrooms and cheese over the omelette, fold it over and transfer to a warm plate.

4 Repeat to make three more omelettes in the same way and serve immediately.

omelettes, tortillas and fritattas

Flat tortillas from Spain, flan-like frittatas from Italy and folded omelettes from France and Thailand – the whole world loves to crack an egg for omelettes.

Thai Chicken Omelette

Preparation and cooking time: 30 minutes
Serves 4

8 large Lion Quality eggs
3 tablespoons chopped fresh coriander
2 skinless, boneless chicken breasts
2 tablespoons vegetable oil
2.5 cm (1-inch) piece root ginger, grated
1 garlic clove, crushed
8 spring onions, sliced
2 carrots, cut into thin sticks
75 g (2¾ oz) bean sprouts
1 tablespoon dark soy sauce
1 teaspoon caster sugar

1 Beat the eggs together with the coriander and set aside. Place the chicken on a board, cover with cling film and bash with a rolling pin until 1 cm (½ inch) thick. Cut into thin strips.
2 Heat half the oil and fry the chicken over a high heat for 5 minutes or until golden. Add the remaining ingredients (except the oil) and stir-fry for 3 minutes. Transfer to a plate and keep warm.
3 Wipe out the frying pan, add a little more oil and when hot pour in a quarter of the egg mixture. Cook for a few seconds until the base has set. Now use a spatula to push the cooked egg towards the centre of the pan, allowing the uncooked egg to run and re-cover the base. Repeat until there is no more runny egg.
4 Continue to cook the omelette for 1–2 minutes or until the base is golden. Remove from the pan and keep warm. Repeat these stages to make four omelettes.
5 Spoon the chicken mixture into the centre of the omelettes. Fold over the edges and turn over to make neat square parcels. Serve warm.

Stilton Soufflé Omelette with Port and Cranberry Sauce

Preparation and cooking time: 20 minutes
Serves 1

2 large Lion Quality eggs, separated
¼ teaspoon mustard powder
15 g (½ oz) butter
salt and freshly ground black pepper

FOR THE FILLING
50 g (1¾ oz) Stilton cheese, sliced
15 g (½ oz) walnut pieces

FOR THE SAUCE
2 tablespoons ready-made cranberry sauce
1 tablespoon port
½ teaspoon finely grated orange zest (optional)

1 Preheat the grill. Mix all the sauce ingredients together and set aside.
2 Beat the egg yolks with 2 tablespoons of water, the mustard, and some seasoning. In a grease-free bowl whisk the egg whites until just stiff. Gently fold the whites into the yolk mixture.
3 Melt the butter in a medium omelette pan. Pour in the egg mixture and cook over a moderate heat until the underside of the omelette is set and pale golden brown. Place the pan under the hot grill and cook for 1–2 minutes or until the top of the omelette is set.
4 Scatter the cheese and walnuts in the centre of the omelette and then fold it in half. Serve immediately on a warm plate with the port and cranberry sauce.

Potato, Tuna and Red Onion Frittata

Preparation and cooking time: 30 minutes
Serves 2–4

350 g (12 oz) new potatoes, sliced
2 tablespoons olive oil
1 red onion, sliced
1 garlic clove, crushed
6 large Lion Quality eggs
3 tablespoons snipped fresh basil
50 g (1¾ oz) freshly grated Parmesan cheese
salt and freshly ground black pepper
200 g can tuna steak in brine, drained and flaked

1 Put the potatoes in a pan of cold water, bring to the boil and cook for 3–4 minutes until just tender. Drain.
2 Heat the oil in a large non-stick frying pan. Add the onion and cook for 3–4 minutes or until softened. Add the garlic and potatoes and cook for a further 2 minutes, stirring.
3 Beat the eggs with the basil, half the cheese and some salt and pepper.
4 Add the tuna to the pan and pour over the egg mixture. Reduce the heat and cook over a low heat for about 15 minutes until the frittata is set but the top is still a bit runny.
5 Preheat the grill to medium. Sprinkle over the remaining cheese and cook under a medium grill for 2–3 minutes or until the top has set and is pale golden. Serve warm or cold, cut into wedges with a salad.

Spanish Pepper and Ham Tortilla

Preparation and cooking time: 20 minutes
Serves 4

3 tablespoons olive oil
1 large onion, sliced
2 red peppers, de-seeded and chopped
2 tablespoons fresh chopped flat-leaf parsley
6 large Lion Quality eggs
a pinch of ground saffron
4 slices Serrano ham, sliced
salt and freshly ground black pepper

1 Heat the oil in a medium non-stick frying pan, add the onion and peppers and cook for 5 minutes or until soft and golden. Stir in the parsley.
2 Beat the eggs and saffron together with salt and pepper. Pour into the pan, and cook over a medium heat, stirring occasionally until most of the egg has set.
3 Stir in the ham. Place the tortilla under a medium hot grill. Cook for a further 4–5 minutes or until the top is golden brown and set. Serve warm or cold in wedges.

Tip: You can use Parma ham or prosciutto instead of Serrano ham. They are all air-dried hams which taste delicious in this tortilla.

Spicy Pepper and Egg Salad

Preparation and cooking time: 20 minutes
Serves 4

6 large Lion Quality eggs
1 Sweet Romaine or Cos lettuce, torn in pieces
6 small tomatoes, quartered
1 red onion, sliced
100 g (3½ oz) salami di Milano, quartered
2 tablespoons capers, drained
350 g (12 oz) new potatoes, halved and cooked
175 g (6 oz) green beans, cooked

FOR THE DRESSING
4 tablespoons olive oil
2 tablespoons balsamic vinegar
1 small garlic clove, crushed
½ teaspoon Tabasco sauce
a pinch of sugar
salt and freshly ground black pepper

1 Place the eggs in a medium pan and cover with cold water. Bring to the boil and boil for 7 minutes. Drain, rinse in cold water, tapping shells all over. Peel and quarter.
2 Tear the lettuce into pieces and place in a large salad bowl. Add the tomatoes, onion, salami, capers, eggs, potatoes and beans.
3 Whisk the dressing ingredients together. Drizzle the dressing over the salad just before serving.

Salad Niçoise

Preparation and cooking time: 25 minutes
Serves 4

4 large Lion Quality eggs
450 g (1 lb) small new potatoes, scrubbed
150 g (5½ oz) fine green beans
200 g can tuna steak in brine, drained
4 tomatoes, quartered
50 g (1¾ oz) black olives
4 teaspoons capers, drained
2 Little Gem lettuces, separated into leaves
Parmesan cheese shavings, to serve

FOR THE DRESSING
4 tablespoons mayonnaise
1 tablespoon freshly grated Parmesan cheese
1 small garlic clove, crushed

1 Place the eggs in a small pan and cover with cold water. Bring to the boil and simmer for 7 minutes. Drain, and rinse in cold water. Shell and quarter the eggs.
2 Cook the potatoes in a large pan of boiling water for 5 minutes. Add the green beans and cook for a further 5 minutes. When the potatoes and beans are tender, drain them under cold running water and place in a salad bowl.
3 Add tuna, tomatoes, olives, capers and lettuce leaves to the salad bowl and toss gently together. Arrange the eggs on top of the salad.
4 To make the dressing, mix the mayonnaise, Parmesan and garlic with 4 tablespoons of cold water. Drizzle over the salad. Scatter with a few Parmesan shavings and serve.

salads

Forget limp lettuce and diets – salads are to be enjoyed! Bursting with flavour, colour and crunch, all of these salads will fit the bill.

Pesto, Egg and Rocket Salad

Preparation and cooking time: 30 minutes
Serves 4

280 g packet white pizza dough mix
flour, for dusting
6 large Lion Quality eggs
225 g packet baby spinach
30 g packet rocket
200 g can tuna steak in brine, drained
100 g (3½ oz) cherry tomatoes, halved
50 g (1¾ oz) pine nuts, toasted

FOR THE DRESSING
1 garlic clove, halved
4 tablespoons extra virgin olive oil
2 tablespoons white wine vinegar
1 tablespoon pesto sauce
½ teaspoon caster sugar
salt and freshly ground black pepper

1 Preheat the oven to Gas Mark 6/200°C/400°F.
2 Make up the pizza mix according to the instructions. Roll the dough into 12 walnut-sized balls. Cover and leave to rise for 10 minutes.
3 Dust with flour and bake in the oven for 7–8 minutes until pale golden and risen.
4 Place the eggs in a medium pan and cover with cold water. Bring to the boil and simmer for 7 minutes. Drain, and rinse in cold water, tapping shells all over. Shell and halve the eggs.
5 Place the spinach and rocket leaves in a large salad bowl. Break the tuna into large chunks and add to the salad bowl with the eggs, tomatoes and pine nuts.
6 Put the dressing ingredients in a screwtop jar and shake well. When ready to serve, remove the garlic with a fork and discard. Pour the dressing over the salad and toss to mix. Serve with the dough balls.

Egg Caesar Salad

Preparation and cooking time: 20 minutes
Serves 4

6 large Lion Quality eggs
3 tablespoons olive oil
100 g (3½ oz) crusty white bread, cubed
1 garlic clove, halved
1 Sweet Romaine or Cos lettuce
50 g can anchovy fillets in oil
25 g (1 oz) freshly grated Parmesan

FOR THE DRESSING
4 tablespoons olive oil
juice of ½ lemon
½ teaspoon caster sugar
½ teaspoon Dijon mustard
½ teaspoon Worcestershire sauce
salt and freshly ground black pepper

1 Place the eggs in a medium pan, cover with cold water. Bring to the boil and boil for 7 minutes. Drain and rinse in cold water, tapping the shells all over. When cold, peel and quarter. Place one egg in a food processor.
2 Meanwhile for the croûtons, heat the oil in a frying pan. Add the bread cubes and garlic and fry for 4–5 minutes over a medium heat, stirring until the croûtons are crisp and golden. Drain on kitchen paper and discard the garlic.
3 Tear the lettuce into large pieces and place in a salad bowl. Drain the anchovies, reserving 2 tablespoons of the oil for the dressing. Dice the anchovies and add to the bowl with the eggs and Parmesan cheese.
4 Place all the dressing ingredients into the food processor with the egg and anchovy oil and whizz together until you have a smooth dressing. Season to taste. Drizzle the dressing over the salad and serve immediately.

Warm Mackerel and Fennel Salad

Preparation and cooking time: 30 minutes
Serves 4

675 g (1½ lb) old potatoes, peeled and cubed
1 tablespoon olive oil
2 fennel bulbs, sliced
a bunch of spring onions, sliced
4 tablespoons Greek yogurt
zest and juice of ½ lemon
3 peppered smoked mackerel fillets
a dash of vinegar
4 large Lion Quality eggs
salad leaves, to serve
salt and freshly ground black pepper

1 Place the potatoes in a large pan, cover with boiling water and simmer for 5 minutes or until just tender. Drain in a colander and rinse in cold water until cool. Leave to drain.
2 Heat the oil in a frying pan, add the fennel and cook for 4–5 minutes, stirring until pale golden. Remove from heat.
3 Place the spring onions, yogurt and lemon zest and juice in a large bowl and mix with a fork. Add the potatoes and fennel. Break the mackerel into chunks, discarding the skin and bones. Add to the bowl and toss together lightly.
4 Fill a large frying pan with salted water, add the vinegar and bring to the boil. Poach the eggs in the simmering water for 3–5 minutes until cooked to your liking. Have a bowl of cold water ready. Use a slotted spoon to lift the eggs from the pan and place them in the cold water. Leave for 1 minute and then drain on kitchen paper.
5 To serve, arrange a few salad leaves on four plates, top with the potato and mackerel salad and place a poached egg on top.

Eggy Rice and Bean Salad

Preparation time: 15 minutes + 15 minutes cooking
Serves 4

6 large Lion Quality eggs
175 g (6 oz) mixed basmati and wild rice
100 g (3½ oz) frozen peas
400 g can mixed pulses, drained
1 red onion, sliced finely
3 tablespoons chopped fresh coriander
salad leaves, to serve

FOR THE DRESSING
6 tablespoons olive oil
3 tablespoons red wine vinegar
½ teaspoon Dijon mustard
½ teaspoon caster sugar
salt and freshly ground black pepper

1 Place the eggs in a medium pan, cover with cold water and bring to the boil. Boil for 7 minutes and then drain and rinse in cold water, tapping the shells all over. When cold, peel away the shells and roughly chop.
2 Meanwhile, cook the rice in boiling salted water for 15 minutes or according to packet instructions. Add the peas and return to the boil. Drain in a sieve, rinse with cold water and drain.
3 In a large bowl, whisk all the dressing ingredients together with a fork and season to taste. Add the rice, pulses, onion, coriander and eggs and toss well to mix. Serve with salad leaves.

Spinach and Ricotta Pancakes

Preparation time: 15 minutes + 25–30 minutes cooking
Serves 4

2 tablespoons olive oil
1 small onion, chopped
1 garlic clove, crushed
350 g (12 oz) young spinach leaves
250 g tub ricotta cheese
½ teaspoon grated nutmeg
50 g (1¾ oz) freshly grated Parmesan
8 pancakes, made according to recipe for Crêpes Suzette, page 38
350 g jar or tub of tomato and herb pasta sauce
150 g pack mozzarella, drained and sliced
salt and freshly ground black pepper

1 Preheat the oven to Gas Mark 6/200°C/400°F. Heat the oil in a large pan, add the onion and garlic and fry for 2–3 minutes. Add the spinach. Cover and cook for 3–4 minutes or until the leaves have wilted. Transfer to a sieve and squeeze out the excess liquid. Return to the pan, beat in the ricotta, nutmeg, half the Parmesan and plenty of salt and pepper.

2 Lay the pancakes out and spoon the spinach in a line down the centre. Roll up and place in a shallow ovenproof dish.

3 Spoon the tomato sauce over the pancakes and place the mozzarella on top. Scatter with Parmesan and bake for 20–25 minutes or until golden and crisp.

Salmon and Egg Pancakes

Preparation time: 10 minutes + 30 minutes cooking
Serves 4

4 pancakes, (one half of recipe for Crêpes Suzette, page 38)
350 g (12 oz) salmon fillets, skinned
4 large Lion Quality eggs
300 ml (½ pint) milk
50 g (1¾ oz) butter
4 tablespoons plain flour
3 tablespoons snipped fresh chives
salt and freshly ground black pepper

1 Preheat the oven to Gas Mark 4/180°C/350°F.

2 Place the salmon in a non-stick frying pan, cover with water and bring to the boil. Cover and gently simmer for 4–5 minutes or until the fish flakes easily. Drain and flake.

3 Put the eggs in a small pan, cover with cold water and bring to the boil. Simmer for 6 minutes and then drain and rinse in cold water, tapping the shells. Peel the eggs and chop. Set aside.

4 Put the milk, butter and flour in a medium pan and bring to the boil, whisking all the time until the mixture boils and thickens. Simmer for 1 minute. Remove from the heat and add the salmon, eggs, chives and salt and pepper to taste. Divide the warm mixture between the pancakes and fold into quarters.

pancakes

Whether sweet or savoury, pancakes deserve more than an annual outing on Shrove Tuesday – pancakes are a flipping treat all year round.

Orange, Pecan and Maple Pancakes

**Preparation and cooking time: 35 minutes +
  20 minutes standing**
Serves 4

4 oranges
175 g (6 oz) plain flour
1½ teaspoons baking powder
1 teaspoon ground cinnamon
4 tablespoons caster sugar
2 large Lion Quality eggs
200 ml (7 fl oz) milk
75 g (3 oz) raisins
a little oil for frying
1 teaspoon arrowroot
50 g (1¾ oz) pecan nuts
4 tablespoons maple syrup

1 Finely grate the zest of 1 orange into a large bowl. Sift over the flour, baking powder and cinnamon, and stir in the sugar. Beat the eggs and milk into the dry ingredients to make a thick, smooth batter. Stir in the raisins. Leave to stand for 20 minutes.
2 Heat a frying pan, brush with oil, then pour in two or three 2-tablespoon heaps of batter. Cook over a medium heat for 2 minutes or until bubbles form on the surface of the pancakes and they are golden underneath. Flip them over and cook for a further 2 minutes. Repeat to make twelve.
3 Pare the zest from the remaining oranges. Cut away the skin and pith and cut the flesh into segments. Place in a pan with any juices. Blend the arrowroot to a smooth paste with a little cold water. Add it to the pan with the pecans and maple syrup. Bring to the boil, stirring, until the sauce thickens.
4 Serve the pancakes warm with the orange sauce.

Crêpes Suzette

**Preparation and cooking time: 35 minutes +
  30 minutes standing time**
Serves 4

FOR THE PANCAKES (MAKES 8)
125 g (4½ oz) plain flour
a pinch of salt
2 large Lion Quality eggs
300 ml (½ pint) milk
oil for cooking

FOR THE ORANGE SAUCE
75 g (2¾ oz) butter
75 g (2¾ oz) sugar
grated zest and juice of 2 oranges
2 oranges, peeled and segmented
2 tablespoons orange-flavoured liqueur
1 tablespoon brandy

1 To make the pancakes sift the flour and salt into a bowl. Make a well in the centre and add the eggs and a little milk. Beat until a smooth paste is formed and then add the remaining milk. Leave to stand for 30 minutes.
2 Heat a little oil in a 15 cm (6-inch) omelette pan. Pour in 2 tablespoons of batter and tilt to coat the base evenly. Cook over a medium heat for 2 minutes, turning once until golden on both sides. Keep warm while you make 7 more pancakes.
3 For the sauce put the butter, sugar, orange zest and juice into a frying pan. Heat until bubbling. Dip each crêpe in the sauce, fold into quarters and arrange in a warm serving dish with the orange segments. Pour the liqueur and brandy into the pan and light with a match. Pour the flaming sauce over the crêpes and serve.

Wild Mushroom and Asparagus Carbonara

Preparation and cooking time: 20 minutes
Serves 2

25 g (1 oz) butter
2 shallots, chopped
100 g (3½ oz) asparagus tips, quartered
1 garlic clove, crushed
225 g (8 oz) mixed mushrooms, sliced
1 tablespoon chopped fresh thyme
150 ml (¼ pint) double cream
4 large Lion Quality eggs, beaten
150 g (5½ oz) quick-cook spaghetti
salt and freshly ground black pepper
freshly grated Parmesan, to serve

1 Melt the butter in a large pan and add the shallots, asparagus and garlic. Cook, stirring, for 5 minutes. Add the mushrooms and thyme and continue to cook, stirring, for another 5 minutes.
2 Beat the cream with the eggs and some seasoning.
3 Cook the spaghetti according to packet instructions.
4 Add the spaghetti to the mushrooms pan, stir in the egg mixture and place over a low heat. Gently cook, stirring all the while, until the sauce thickens slightly and coats the pasta. Season to taste and serve hot, sprinkled with Parmesan cheese.

Seafood and Egg Pasta

Preparation and cooking time: 20–25 minutes
Serves 4

175 g (6 oz) pasta bows
4 large Lion Quality eggs
6 tablespoons olive oil
3 tablespoons pesto sauce
2 tablespoons white wine vinegar
1 tablespoon lemon juice
½ teaspoon Dijon mustard
350 g (12 oz) mixed cooked shellfish, thawed
    if frozen
1 onion, chopped finely
salt and freshly ground black pepper
freshly chopped parsley, to garnish

1 Cook the pasta for 8–10 minutes in boiling salted water, or until tender. Rinse in cold water and drain.
2 Put the eggs in a small pan, cover with cold water and bring to the boil. Boil for 7 minutes and then drain and rinse in cold water, tapping the shells all over. When cold peel away the shells and quarter.
3 Place the oil, pesto sauce, white wine vinegar, lemon juice, mustard and seasoning in a large bowl and whisk together with a fork.
4 Add the drained pasta, shellfish, eggs, onion and gently mix together. Serve in bowls garnished with freshly chopped parsley.

pasta

Whatever shape you choose, pasta always makes a great family meal. Teamed with eggs, it's tasty and nutritious too.

Macaroni Cheese with Tomatoes and Egg

Preparation time: 30 minutes + 20–25 minutes cooking
Serves 4

225 g (8 oz) macaroni
100 g (3½ oz) frozen peas
6 large Lion Quality eggs
65 g (2½ oz) butter
225 g (8 oz) cherry tomatoes, halved
1 bunch spring onions, sliced
600 ml (1 pint) milk
3 tablespoons plain flour
1 tablespoon wholegrain mustard
100 g (3½ oz) mature Cheddar, grated
salt and freshly ground black pepper

1 Preheat oven to Gas Mark 6/200°C/400°F. Cook the macaroni in boiling salted water for 7 minutes or according to the pack instructions. Add the peas and return to the boil. Drain in a colander, rinse with cold water, drain again and set aside.
2 Put the eggs in a medium pan, cover with cold water and bring to the boil. Boil for 7 minutes and then drain and rinse in cold water tapping the shells all over. When cold, peel away the shells and roughly chop.
3 Melt 15 g (½ oz) of the butter in a medium pan, add the tomatoes and onions and sauté for 2–3 minutes or until softened. Transfer to a large ovenproof dish.
4 Put the milk, the rest of the butter, flour and mustard in the pan and slowly bring to the boil, whisking all the time until the mixture boils and thickens. Simmer for 1 minute. Stir in half the cheese and season to taste.
5 Pour the sauce over the tomatoes, add the eggs and pasta and toss well to mix. Sprinkle over the remaining cheese and bake for 20–25 minutes or until golden brown. Serve hot.

Roasted Vegetable and Egg Gratin

Preparation time: 30 minutes + 20–25 minutes cooking
Serves 4

350 g (12 oz) pasta shells
6 large Lion Quality eggs
2 small red onions, cut into wedges
1 pack red, green and yellow peppers, de-seeded and cut into chunks
150 g (5 oz) chestnut mushrooms, halved
3 tablespoons olive oil
1 garlic clove, chopped
400 ml tub crème fraîche
4 tablespoons pesto sauce
100 g (3½ oz) Gruyère cheese, grated
salt and freshly ground black pepper

1 Preheat the oven to Gas Mark 6/200°C/400°F. Cook the pasta shells in boiling salted water for 10 minutes or according to the pack instructions. Drain in a colander, rinse with cold water, drain again and set aside.
2 Put the eggs in a medium pan, cover with cold water and bring to the boil. Boil for 7 minutes and then drain and rinse in cold water, tapping the shells all over. When cold, peel away the shells and cut into quarters.
3 Place all the vegetables on the grill tray. Add the oil and garlic and season with salt and ground black pepper. Toss together. Cook under a hot grill for 8–10 minutes, stirring occasionally, until charred around edges.
4 Put the pasta, eggs and vegetables in a large ovenproof dish. Beat the crème fraîche together with the pesto sauce, half the cheese and some seasoning. Add to the pasta and toss well to mix. Sprinkle over the remaining cheese and bake for 20–25 minutes or until golden brown. Serve hot.

Cheddar and Tomato Quiche

**Preparation time: 10 minutes + 1 hour 10 minutes
   cooking**
Serves 8–10

225 g (8 oz) ready-rolled shortcrust pastry
3 tablespoons pesto sauce
175 g (6 oz) mature Cheddar, grated
5 large Lion Quality eggs
500 g tub crème fraîche
4 tablespoons freshly snipped chives
4 plum tomatoes, sliced lengthways
1 tablespoon olive oil
salt and freshly ground black pepper

1 Preheat the oven to Gas Mark 6/200°C/400°F. Use the pastry to line a 20 cm (8-inch) fluted deep flan tin. Trim the edges, line the base with greaseproof paper and fill with baking beans. Bake for 20 minutes, removing the beans for the final 5 minutes.

2 Spread the pesto sauce over the base and scatter over a third of the Cheddar. Beat the eggs, crème fraîche, chives and seasoning together, and stir in the remaining cheese. Pour into the pastry case and bake for 20 minutes or until the filling is beginning to set.

3 Arrange the sliced tomatoes on top of the quiche, overlapping them slightly. Brush with the oil and bake for a further 30 minutes. Serve warm or cold.

Egg, Bacon and Potato Bake

**Preparation time: 20 minutes + 1 hour 15 minutes
   baking**
Serves 6

900 g (2 lb) potatoes, sliced thinly
1 large onion, sliced and separated into rings
2 tablespoons oil
15 g (½ oz) butter
225 g (8 oz) smoked pork sausage, sliced
4 back bacon rashers, de-rinded and cut into strips
2 tablespoons freshly chopped parsley
2 large Lion Quality eggs
150 ml (¼ pint) milk
salt and freshly ground black pepper

1 Preheat the oven to Gas Mark 4/180°C/350°F.
2 Parboil the potatoes for 3 minutes and drain. Gently fry the onion in oil for 5 minutes. Butter a 1.5-litre (2½-pint) ovenproof dish.

3 Layer the potatoes, onion, sausage, bacon and parsley in the dish. Add some seasoning as you go and end with a layer of potatoes. Beat the eggs and milk together and pour over the potatoes. Cover with lightly oiled foil. Bake for 1 hour 15 minutes until the potatoes are tender. Remove the foil for the last 10 minutes of cooking to allow the potatoes to turn golden.

suppers

Eggs are a brilliant ingredient around which to base a tasty evening meal. Try them in these special recipes perfect for a casual supper with friends or family.

Rosti Nests with Smoked Salmon and Eggs

Preparation and cooking time: 25 minutes
Serves 4

450 g (1 lb) old potatoes, peeled
3 tablespoons freshly snipped chives
175 g (6 oz) smoked salmon
2 tablespoons vegetable oil
50 g (2 oz) butter
a dash of vinegar
4 large Lion Quality eggs
salt and freshly ground black pepper
small bunch of watercress, to serve

1 Place the whole peeled potatoes in a large pan, cover with water and bring to the boil. Cover and simmer for 5 minutes or until a little tender. Drain and rinse in cold water. When the potatoes are cool enough to handle, drain again and then coarsely grate them into a large bowl. Add the chives and plenty of salt and pepper. Chop half the salmon and stir into the potatoes.
2 Heat half the oil and butter in a large non-stick frying pan. Divide the grated potato into four and add to the pan, two portions at a time. Shape the portions into rounds and cook for 6–8 minutes, turning once, until golden brown on both sides.
3 Fill a large frying pan with salted water, add the vinegar and bring to the boil. Poach the eggs in the simmering water for 3–5 minutes depending how you like your eggs cooked.
4 To serve, divide the watercress between four serving plates, top with the rosti cakes, the remaining salmon and finally the poached egg. Serve immediately.

Chorizo, Egg and Leek Mash

Preparation time: 10 minutes + 15 minutes cooking
Serves 4

1 kg (2 lb 4 oz) potatoes, cut into even-sized chunks
4 large Lion Quality eggs
1 tablespoon olive oil
1 garlic clove, crushed
3 leeks, sliced
75 g (3 oz) chorizo sausage, sliced
5–7 tablespoons milk
salt and freshly ground black pepper
sprigs of flat-leaf parsley, to garnish

1 Cook the potatoes in a large pan of boiling water for 12–15 minutes or until soft. Drain and mash with the milk and some seasoning. Keep warm.
2 Meanwhile put the eggs in a small pan, cover with cold water and bring to the boil. Boil for 7 minutes and then drain and rinse in cold water, tapping the shells all over. When cold enough to handle, peel and chop.
3 Heat the oil in a small frying pan and cook the garlic and leeks for 5–6 minutes, stirring regularly, until tender and lightly browned. Grill the chorizo under a hot grill for 1–2 minutes until crisp.
4 Spoon mashed potato onto four warmed plates. Top with the sautéed leeks, chopped hard-boiled egg and crisp chorizo. Garnish with flat-leaf parsley.

Healthier Ham, Egg and Chips

Preparation time: 15 minutes + 35 minutes cooking
Serves 4

675 g (1½ lb) potatoes, scrubbed and cut into
   thick wedges
3 tablespoons vegetable oil
4 lean bacon chops, any fat snipped at even
   intervals
2 tomatoes, halved
4 large Lion Quality eggs
salt and freshly ground black pepper

1 Preheat the oven to Gas Mark 6/200°C/400°F. Toss
the potatoes in the oil and season lightly with salt and
pepper. Transfer to a large roasting tin and bake for 20
minutes, turning halfway through the cooking time.
2 Give the tin a good shake and move the potatoes to
one end. Add the bacon chops and return to the oven
for a further 8 minutes. Turn the chops, add the tomato
halves and break the eggs into the tin. Sprinkle with a
little black pepper. Return to the oven for 3–5 minutes
or until the bacon is cooked and the eggs are just set.

Baked Eggs in Spinach Tarts

Preparation time: 30 minutes + 30 minutes cooking
Serves 6

450 g (1 lb) ready-made shortcrust pastry
2 tablespoons olive oil
1 small onion, chopped
1 garlic clove
350 g (12 oz) young spinach leaves, washed
½ teaspoon grated nutmeg
4 tablespoons crème fraîche
7 large Lion Quality eggs
50 g (1¾ oz) Gruyère cheese, grated
salt and freshly ground black pepper

1 Preheat the oven to Gas Mark 6/200°C/400°F. Cut
the pastry into six pieces and roll each out thinly on a
lightly floured board. Use to line six 10 cm (4-inch)
fluted flan tins. Line with greaseproof paper and half fill
with baking beans. Bake for 10 minutes. Remove the
paper and beans and bake for a further 5 minutes.
2 Meanwhile, heat the oil in a large pan, fry the onion
and garlic for 2–3 minutes or until soft, then add the
spinach leaves, stirring to pack them into the pan.
Cover and cook over a medium heat for 2–3 minutes
or until all the leaves have wilted.
3 Tip the spinach into a sieve and squeeze out the
excess liquid. Return to the pan. Add the nutmeg, 2
tablespoons of crème fraîche, 1 beaten egg, half the
cheese and plenty of salt and pepper. Mix well.
4 Divide the spinach between the pastry cases, making
a well in the centre of each. Carefully crack an egg into
each tart, spoon a teaspoon of crème fraîche over each
and sprinkle on the remaining cheese. Bake for 12–15
minutes or until the tops are pale golden, the eggs just
set and the yolks still a little runny.

Fish with Poached Egg

Preparation time: 10 minutes + 10 minutes cooking
Serves 2

4 plum tomatoes, sliced
12 fresh basil leaves
1 tablespoon balsamic vinegar
2 tablespoons extra-virgin olive oil
2 × 150 g (5½ oz) thick fillets of fresh white fish,
   skinned
a dash of vinegar
2 large Lion Quality eggs
freshly ground black pepper
sprigs of fresh parsley, to garnish

1 Preheat the oven to Gas Mark 6/200°C/400°F. Lightly oil a small ovenproof dish. Arrange the tomatoes and basil leaves in two heaps. Season with a dash of balsamic vinegar and some ground black pepper. Drizzle with a little oil and top the tomatoes with the fish.
2 Season the fish and drizzle with remaining oil. Bake for 10 minutes.
3 Fill a large frying pan with salted water, add the vinegar and bring to the boil. Poach the eggs in the simmering water for 3–5 minutes.
4 Remove the fish from the oven and set on two warmed plates. Top with the poached eggs and garnish with parsley.

Kedgeree

Preparation time: 10 minutes + 15–20 minutes cooking
Serves 4

4 cardamom pods, split
225 g (8 oz) basmati rice
75 g (2¾ oz) frozen peas
6 large Lion Quality eggs
350 g (12 oz) salmon fillet
25 g (1 oz) butter
a bunch of spring onions, sliced
1 tablespoon medium curry paste
3 tablespoons crème fraîche
4 tablespoons freshly chopped parsley
salt and freshly ground black pepper

1 Bring a large pan of salted water to the boil and add the cardamom pods. Add the rice and simmer for 5 minutes. Add the peas and simmer for 2 minutes.
2 Boil the eggs in a medium pan for 6 minutes (page 6). Drain and rinse in cold water, tapping the shells all over. Peel and quarter.
3 Put the salmon in the frying pan, skin-side up. Add enough water just to cover, slowly bring to the boil and cover and simmer for 3–4 minutes or until just cooked. Drain and flake the flesh.
4 Melt the butter in a medium pan, add the spring onions and curry paste and cook for 1 minute. Stir in the rice, salmon, crème fraîche and half the parsley. Season well. Serve topped with the eggs and garnished with the remaining parsley.

eggs with fish

There's something about this classic combination that is especially good. Our four recipes are no exception – perfect for a special meal.

Haddock and Egg Florentine

Preparation time: 20 minutes + 20 minutes cooking
Serves 4

225 g bag young spinach leaves
50 g (1¾ oz) butter
4 tomatoes, sliced
4 × 175 g (6 oz) smoked haddock fillets
2 tablespoons plain flour
300 ml (½ pint) milk
50 g (1¾ oz) Cheddar cheese, grated
4 large Lion Quality eggs
salt and freshly ground black pepper

1 Preheat the oven to Gas Mark 4/180°C/350°F.
2 Empty the spinach into a large pan, cover and cook for 2–3 minutes or until wilted. Drain well in a sieve, pressing down with a wooden spoon to remove the excess juices. Add 15 g (½ oz) butter and season to taste. Arrange four heaps of spinach in a shallow ovenproof dish. Top with the sliced tomatoes, then the haddock fillets on top of the spinach. Cover with buttered foil and bake for 15–20 minutes or until the fish flakes easily.
2 Meanwhile, place the remaining butter, flour and milk in a medium pan and bring to the boil, whisking all the time, until the mixture boils and thickens. Cook for 1 minute and then remove from the heat. Stir in half the cheese and set aside.
4 Preheat the grill. Top each fillet with a poached egg, pour over the sauce and top with the remaining cheese. Cook for 2 minutes under a hot grill until golden brown.

Salmon and Egg Fishcakes with Lemon Sauce

Preparation time: 30 minutes + 30 minutes cooking
Serves 4

350 g (12 oz) salmon fillet, skinned
7 large Lion Quality eggs
675 g (1½ lb) mashed potato
2 tablespoons freshly chopped tarragon
4 tablespoons plain flour
100 g (3½ oz) natural dried breadcrumbs
4 tablespoons vegetable oil
50 g (1¾ oz) butter, melted
grated zest and juice of 1 small lemon
salt and freshly ground black pepper

1 Place the salmon in a frying pan, add water to just cover and bring to the boil. Cover and simmer for 5–6 minutes or until the fish flakes easily. Transfer to a plate and flake the flesh with a fork.
2 Place 4 eggs in a pan, cover with cold water and bring to the boil. Simmer for 7 minutes. Drain, rinse in cold water, tapping the shells. Peel and chop roughly.
3 Mix together the mashed potato, tarragon, salmon and boiled eggs with some seasoning and a beaten egg. Divide the mixture into eight and shape into round patties.
4 Beat another egg in a shallow dish. Coat the cakes first in the flour, then egg and then breadcrumbs, turning them until well coated. Chill until required.
5 Heat the oil in a large frying pan, add the fish cakes and cook over a medium heat for 8–10 minutes, turning once until golden on all sides. Keep warm.
6 To make the sauce, place the remaining egg, the butter, lemon zest and juice and some seasoning in a heatproof bowl. Place the bowl over a pan of simmering water. Use an electric whisk to whisk for 2–3 minutes or until thick. Serve the fishcakes hot with the sauce.

Chorizo and Potato Sizzle

Preparation and cooking time: 30 minutes
Serves 4

4 tablespoons olive oil
450 g (1 lb) new potatoes, halved
2 small red onions, cut into thin wedges
175 g (6 oz) chorizo sausage, sliced
225 g (8 oz) cherry tomatoes, halved
2 tablespoons chopped flat-leaf parsley
1 tablespoon red wine vinegar
4 large Lion Quality eggs
salt and freshly ground black pepper

1 Heat half the oil in a large non-stick frying pan, add the potatoes and cook over a medium heat for 10 minutes or until golden. Remove from the pan with a slotted spoon. Drain on kitchen paper and keep warm.
2 Add the onions and chorizo to the pan and cook, stirring, for 4 minutes. Stir in the tomatoes, parsley, potatoes and vinegar, and season with black pepper. Transfer to a dish and keep warm.
3 Wipe out the pan, add the remaining oil and when it is hot carefully crack the eggs into the pan. Fry the eggs over a medium heat (page 6).
4 To serve, divide the potato mixture between four warm plates and top each with a fried egg.

Sausage and Egg Pie

Preparation time: 25 minutes + 30–35 minutes cooking
Serves 8

350 g (12 oz) ready-made shortcrust pastry
4 teaspoons wholegrain mustard
900 g (2 lb) good quality sausagemeat
1 bunch spring onions, sliced
1 teaspoon mixed dried herbs
4 large Lion Quality eggs

1 Preheat the oven to Gas Mark 6/200°C/400°F. Roll out two thirds of the pastry thinly and use to line the base and sides of a 20 cm (8-inch) deep, loose-based cake tin. Trim the pastry level with the top of the tin. Brush the pastry with 3 teaspoons of the mustard.
2 Mix the sausagemeat with the spring onions and herbs and spoon two thirds into the tin. Make 4 deep holes, cracking an egg into each. Cover with the remaining sausagemeat, pressing it down firmly around the edges.
3 Roll out the remaining pastry thinly and cut out a 20 cm (8-inch) round using the cake tin as a guide. Brush with the remaining mustard and place mustard-side-down on top of the sausagemeat. Brush the top with beaten egg. Fold the top edge of the pastry wall over the lid and crimp to seal. Make a steam hole in the centre and use any trimmings to make decorations for the lid. Brush with the remaining egg.
4 Stand the pie on a baking sheet and bake for 30–35 minutes or until golden brown. Leave to cool in the tin for 15 minutes before cutting into wedges to serve warm. Alternatively, cool and chill and serve with salad.

family meals

Cooking meals the whole family will enjoy is always a challenge, but with a few eggs and a little imagination, you'll have empty plates all round

Prawn and Egg Chow Mein

Preparation and cooking time: 15 minutes
Serves 4

225 g (8 oz) medium egg noodles
2 tablespoons vegetable oil
1 bunch spring onions, cut into strips
1 carrot, grated
100 g (3½ oz) mange-tout, shredded
225 g (8 oz) cooked, peeled tiger prawns
1 garlic clove, crushed
2.5 cm (1-inch) piece root ginger, grated
1 large red chilli, de-seeded and chopped
4 large Lion Quality eggs, beaten
2 tablespoons dark soy sauce

1 Cook the noodles according to the packet instructions, drain and set aside. Heat half the oil in a large wok, add the spring onions, carrot, mange-tout, prawns, garlic, ginger and chilli. Stir-fry for 2–3 minutes. Transfer to a bowl and keep warm.
2 Add the remaining oil to the wok and pour in the eggs. Cook, stirring continuously, until the eggs have scrambled.
3 Add the soy sauce, noodles and stir-fried vegetables to the wok and stir-fry together for 1 minute. Serve immediately in bowls.

Vegetable and Egg Curry

Preparation time: 25 minutes + 15–20 minutes cooking
Serves 4

6 large Lion Quality eggs
2 tablespoons vegetable oil
1 onion, chopped
450 g (1 lb) sweet potatoes, peeled and cubed
1 garlic clove, crushed
2.5 cm (1-inch) piece root ginger, grated
225 g (8 oz) green lentils
4 tablespoons medium curry paste
400 g can coconut milk
1 vegetable stock cube
350 g (12 oz) young spinach leaves
salt and freshly ground black pepper
rice and naan bread, to serve

1 Put the eggs in a medium pan, cover with cold water and bring to the boil. Boil for 7 minutes and then drain and rinse in cold water, tapping the shells all over. When cold, peel away the shells and cut into halves and set aside.
2 Heat the oil in a large pan, add the onion and sweet potatoes and sauté for 5 minutes until golden. Add the garlic, ginger, lentils and curry paste and fry for 30 seconds.
3 Add the coconut milk, stock cube and 150 ml (¼ pint) water. Bring to the boil, cover and simmer for 15–20 minutes or until the lentils and potatoes are tender. Stir in the spinach.
4 When the leaves have wilted, season to taste. Place the halved eggs on top of the curry, cover and cook for 2–3 minutes to heat through the eggs. Serve immediately with rice and naan bread.

Dolcelatte Gougère

Preparation time: 25 minutes + 25–30 minutes baking
Serves 4

100 g (3½ oz) plain flour
a pinch of salt and cayenne pepper
75 g (2¾ oz) butter
3 large Lion Quality eggs, beaten
25 g (1 oz) Parmesan, grated
100 g (3½ oz) Dolcelatte or other blue cheese, diced
2 tablespoons olive oil
1 red onion, sliced
1 red pepper, de-seeded and sliced
1 garlic clove, crushed
4 tomatoes, chopped
4 tablespoons dry white wine
2 tablespoons sun-dried tomato paste
400 g can artichoke hearts, halved
3 tablespoons snipped fresh basil leaves
½ teaspoon caster sugar

1 Preheat the oven to Gas Mark 6/200°C/400°F. Lightly oil a large oval or round gratin dish.
2 Sift the flour, salt and cayenne together onto a plate. Melt the butter with 200 ml (7 fl oz) water in a saucepan, then quickly bring to the boil. Remove from the heat, add the flour and beat until lump free. Return to the heat and cook, beating until the mixture is smooth and forms a ball. Cool for 2 minutes.
3 Use an electric whisk to beat in the eggs until the mixture is smooth and shiny. Stir in the Parmesan and half the Dolcelatte. Spoon the mixture around the edges of the dish and bake for 25–30 minutes.
4 Heat the oil in a large frying pan. Add the onions and pepper and sauté for 4 minutes. Add the garlic, tomatoes, wine and tomato paste. Simmer for 5 minutes. Stir in the artichokes, basil and sugar.
5 When the gougère is ready, spoon in the filling and scatter over the remaining Dolcelatte cheese. Return to the oven for 5 minutes or until the cheese has melted.

Toad in the Hole with Onion Gravy

Preparation time: 25 minutes + 30 minutes standing + 30–35 minutes cooking
Serves 4

100 g (3½ oz) plain flour
a pinch of salt
4 large Lion Quality eggs
200 ml (7 fl oz) milk
1 tablespoon vegetable oil
8 premium pork sausages
1 red onion, sliced

FOR THE ONION GRAVY
2 tablespoons vegetable oil
2 onions, sliced
a pinch of sugar
4 teaspoons plain flour
425 ml (¾ pint) beef stock

1 Sift the flour and salt into a large bowl and make a well in the centre. Add the eggs and a little milk and beat until smooth. Gradually beat in the remaining milk to make a batter. Leave to stand for 30 minutes.
2 Preheat the oven to Gas Mark 7/220°C/425°F. Put the oil, sausages and onion into shallow ovenproof dishes or 1 large roasting tin and toss. Bake for 5 minutes.
3 Remove the sausages from the oven, turn them all over, then pour over the batter. Bake for 25–30 minutes or until the batter has risen and is crisp and golden.
4 To make the gravy, heat the oil in a medium pan, add the onions and cook for 5 minutes or until golden brown. Add the sugar and cook over a low heat for 2 minutes or until caramelised.
5 Add the flour to the pan and cook, stirring for 1 minute. Gradually add the stock, then bring to the boil and simmer for 1 minute. Season to taste and keep warm. Serve the toad in the hole with the onion gravy.

Summer Herb Roulade

Preparation time: 10 minutes + 10–12 minutes cooking
Serves 6

oil for greasing
4 large Lion Quality eggs, separated
75 g (2¾ oz) mature Cheddar, grated
75 g (2¾ oz) self-raising flour, sifted
85 g packet of watercress
25 g (1 oz) ground almonds
3 tablespoons freshly grated Parmesan
6 tablespoons garlic mayonnaise
4 tomatoes, halved and sliced thinly
60 g bag of herb salad
salt and freshly ground black pepper

1 Preheat the oven to Gas Mark 6/200°C/400°F. Oil a 33 x 23 cm (13 x 9-inch) Swiss roll tin and line with baking parchment.
2 In a food processor blend the egg yolks, Cheddar, flour, watercress and almonds with some seasoning and 4 tablespoons water until smooth. Whisk the egg whites with a pinch of salt until soft peaks form. Fold in the watercress mixture.
3 Spoon into the tin and level the surface. Bake for 10–12 minutes or until firm. Turn out on a sheet of greaseproof paper sprinkled with Parmesan. Peel off the lining paper and cover with a damp tea towel.
4 When cool, spread with the mayonnaise and scatter over the tomatoes and half the herb salad. Roll up the roulade from one of the short sides. Serve in slices with the remaining herb salad.

Twice Baked Cheese and Chive Soufflés

Preparation time: 20 minutes + 40 minutes cooking
Serves 6

65 g (2½ oz) butter
300 ml (½ pint) milk
50 g (1¾ oz) plain flour
5 large Lion Quality eggs, separated
1 teaspoon Dijon mustard
100 g (3½ oz) mature Cheddar cheese, grated
50 g (1¾ oz) freshly grated Parmesan
15 g pack fresh chives, snipped
150 ml (¼ pint) double cream

1 Preheat the oven to Gas Mark 4/180°C/350°F. Use 15 g (½ oz) butter to grease six 250 ml (9 fl oz) ramekins.
2 Place the milk, remaining butter and flour in a medium pan and gently heat, whisking until the mixture boils and thickens. Simmer for 1 minute. Remove from the heat, beat in the egg yolks, mustard, half the Cheddar and Parmesan and the chives. Season with pepper.
3 Whisk the egg whites until they form stiff peaks. Stir about a third into the cheese sauce and gently fold in the remainder. Divide between the ramekins and stand in a baking tray. Pour boiling water halfway up the sides and bake for 20 minutes or until risen and golden. Leave to cool.
4 Remove from ramekins and place on a baking tray. Pour over the cream and scatter over the remaining cheeses. Bake at Gas Mark 4/180°C/350°F for 20–25 minutes or until re-risen. Serve immediately.

soufflés and roulades

Featherlight and so impressive, soufflés and roulades are easier to make than you think.

Raspberry Cheesecake

Preparation time: 15 minutes + 1 hour baking
Serves 8

50 g (1¾ oz) amaretti biscuits, crushed
100 g (3½ oz) digestive biscuits, crushed
75 g (2¾ oz) butter, melted

FOR THE FILLING
175 g (6 oz) raspberries, thawed if frozen
2 tablespoons icing sugar
2 × 200 g cartons full-fat soft cheese
200 g tub crème fraîche
2 large Lion Quality eggs
zest and juice of 1 small lemon
75 g (2¾ oz) caster sugar
1 tablespoon cornflour
icing sugar, to dust

1 Preheat the oven to Gas Mark 6/200°C/400°F.
2 Grease the base and sides of a 20 cm (8-inch) spring-base cake tin and line with baking parchment.
3 To make the base, mix the biscuits with the butter and spread over the base of the tin. Chill.
4 To make the filling, blend the raspberries in a food processor with the icing sugar and set aside.
5 Rinse out the food processor. Put the remaining ingredients in the food processor and blend until smooth. Pour the mixture over the base, and then spoon over the raspberry purée. Use a skewer to swirl through the mixture to create a marbled effect. Bake for 20 minutes and then reduce the temperature to Gas Mark 4/180°C/ 350°F and bake for a further 40 minutes. Cover the top loosely with foil if it begins to brown too much.
6 Leave to cool in the tin. Remove the sides from the tin and peel off the lining paper. Place the cheesecake on a serving plate. Serve chilled and dusted with icing sugar.

Tropical Fruit Pavlovas

Preparation time: 15 minutes + 1–1½ hours baking
Serves 6

3 large Lion Quality egg whites
175 g (6 oz) caster sugar
1 teaspoon cornflour
1 teaspoon raspberry or white wine vinegar
a few drops vanilla essence

FOR THE FILLING
300 ml (½ pint) double cream
1 mango, peeled, stoned and diced
1 papaya, peeled, de-seeded and diced
2 kiwi fruit, peeled and diced
2 passion fruits, halved

1 Preheat the oven to Gas Mark 1/140°C/275°F. Grease a large baking sheet and line with non-stick baking parchment. Place egg whites in a large, clean bowl and use an electric whisk to whisk them until stiff peaks form.
2 Add about a third of the sugar and whisk again until the egg whites are stiff and shiny. Add the sugar in two more batches whisking in between. When all the sugar has been whisked in the egg whites will be really stiff and shiny. In a small bowl mix the cornflour, vinegar and vanilla together until smooth and then fold into the meringue.
3 Make six heaps of meringue on the baking tray and use the back of a spoon to shape the mixture into nests. Or you could spoon the meringue into a large piping bag fitted with a plain nozzle and pipe six 6 cm (2¼ inch) circles. Then pipe a double layer of meringue around the edge to make the nests. Bake for 1–1½ hours or until the base of the meringue feels dry and crisp when tapped.
4 To finish, whip the cream until it forms soft peaks and spoon into the centre of the meringues. Top with the mango, papaya and kiwi fruits, and spoon over the passion fruit seeds. Serve within an hour of filling.

Crème Caramel

Preparation time: 10 minutes + 25–30 minutes baking + chilling
Makes 6

225 g (8 oz) caster sugar
600 ml (1 pint) milk
1 vanilla pod, split and seeds removed
3 large Lion Quality eggs
3 large Lion Quality egg yolks

1 Preheat the oven to Gas Mark 3/170°C/325°F. Place 175 g (6 oz) of the sugar in a heavy-based pan and place over a low heat. Cook for about 8 minutes, shaking the pan occasionally, until the sugar dissolves and caramelises. Divide between six 175 ml (6 fl oz) ramekins, turning them to spread the caramel over the base.
2 Heat the milk and vanilla pod in the caramel pan until the milk is almost boiling; stir to dissolve the caramel from the sides of the pan. Beat the eggs and egg yolks and remaining sugar together. Add the hot milk. Strain through a sieve back into a clean jug and pour into the ramekins.
3 Place the ramekins in a roasting tin and pour in enough boiling water to come halfway up the sides. Cover the tin with foil and bake for 25–30 minutes or until just set but still a bit wobbly in the middle. Cool and then chill for at least 2 hours.
4 Gently run a knife around the edge of each crème caramel and invert onto a serving plate. Serve with single cream.

To make spun sugar: slowly melt 50 g (1½ oz) caster sugar in a heavy-based pan over a low heat until caramel forms. Remove from the heat and cool slightly. Dip two forks in the caramel, hold them over a baking sheet and quickly draw the forks together, back to back, then apart, so that strands of caramel form and fall off. Repeat, warming the pan of caramel as necessary. Gather six loose balls of spun sugar together and place on top of the desserts.

Cherry Clafoutis

Preparation time: 15 minutes + 30–35 minutes baking
Serves 6

oil for greasing
450 g (1 lb) fresh cherries, pitted or 400 g can pitted black cherries, drained
4 tablespoons kirsch or cherry brandy
100 ml (4 fl oz) milk
150 ml (¼ pint) whipping cream
½ teaspoon vanilla essence
4 large Lion Quality eggs
100 g (3½ oz) caster sugar
25 g (1 oz) plain flour
icing sugar, to dust
whipped cream, to serve

1 Preheat the oven to Gas Mark 6/200°C/400°F. Lightly oil a 23 cm (9-inch) wide ovenproof dish. Mix the cherries and kirsch or brandy together and set aside.
2 Put the milk, cream and vanilla in a pan and heat until almost boiling. In a large bowl, beat the eggs and sugar until creamy, add the flour and beat until smooth. Pour over the hot milk and mix well. You can leave the mixture to stand for up to 1 hour.
3 Scatter the cherries over the base of the dish. Stir the batter, and pour over the cherries. Bake for 30-35 minutes or until risen and puffy. Dust with icing sugar and serve warm or cold with whipped cream.

Lime and Coconut Crunchies

Preparation: 10 minutes + 10–15 minutes baking
Makes 12 biscuits

50 g (1¾ oz) butter, softened
75 g (2¾ oz) icing sugar
zest and juice of 2 limes
1 large Lion Quality egg
100 g (3½ oz) plain flour
¼ teaspoon baking powder
50 g (1¾ oz) desiccated coconut

TO DECORATE
25 g (1 oz) large coconut shreds
65 g (2 oz) icing sugar

1 Preheat the oven to Gas Mark 4/180°C/350°F. Lightly oil two baking sheets.
2 Cream the butter and icing sugar together until fluffy. Reserve 1 tablespoon of the lime juice. Add the remaining lime juice, zest, egg, flour, baking powder, desiccated coconut and mix well to form a soft dough.
3 Place six spoonfuls of the mixture well apart on each of the baking sheets. Flatten with a fork and sprinkle over the coconut shreds. Bake for 10–12 minutes until golden. Cool on a wire rack.
4 To decorate mix the reserved lime juice with the icing sugar to make a thin icing. Drizzle the icing over the biscuits. Leave to set. These biscuits can be stored in an airtight container for up to 3 days.

Hazelnut and Banoffee Swiss Roll

Preparation time: 15 minutes +10–12 minutes cooking
Serves 8

3 large Lion Quality eggs
50 g (1¾ oz) caster sugar + extra for dredging
50 g (1¾ oz) light soft brown sugar
100 g (3½ oz) plain flour
50 g (2 oz) hazelnuts, toasted and chopped
4 tablespoons toffee spread
1 banana, sliced
200 ml (7 fl oz) double cream, whipped

1 Preheat the oven to Gas Mark 6/200°C/400°F. Grease a 33 × 23 cm (13 × 9-inch) Swiss roll tin and line with baking parchment.
2 Put the eggs and two sugars together in a large heatproof bowl over a pan of simmering water. Whisk until the mixture has doubled in size.
3 Remove from the heat and whisk until cool. Fold in the flour with 1 tablespoon water and pour into the tin. Scatter over the hazelnuts. Bake for 10–12 minutes.
4 Place a sheet of greaseproof paper on a damp tea towel and dredge with caster sugar. Turn the cake out onto the paper. Peel away the lining paper, trim off the edges and loosely roll up. Leave to cool.
5 When cold, spread the toffee spread, bananas and cream over the cake. Roll up and serve in slices.

cakes and bakes

Who can resist the smell of home baking? Go on, treat yourself!

Passion Cake Bars

Preparation time: 15 minutes + 35–40 minutes baking
Makes 12 bars

2 large Lion Quality eggs
175 g (6 oz) light soft brown sugar
100 ml (3½ fl oz) sunflower oil
225 g (8 oz) plain flour
2 teaspoons bicarbonate of soda
2 teaspoons ground mixed spice
1 teaspoon baking powder
225 g (8 oz) carrots, grated
100 g (3½ oz) walnuts, chopped
zest and juice of 1 orange

TO DECORATE
1 orange
25 g (1 oz) caster sugar
250 g tub quark or cream cheese
2 tablespoons icing sugar
1 tablespoon clear honey

1 Preheat the oven to Gas Mark 3/170°C/325°F. Lightly oil a rectangular cake tin measuring 17 × 26 × 3.5 cm (6½ × 10¼ × 1⅜ inches). Line the base with baking parchment.
2 In a large bowl whisk the eggs, sugar and oil together with an electric whisk until pale, thick and fluffy. Fold in the remaining ingredients and pour into the prepared tin. Bake for 35–40 minutes until risen and firm to the touch. Cool in the tin.
3 Meanwhile, use a potato peeler to thinly pare the zest from the orange and cut it into matchstick strips. Toss in caster sugar and leave to dry on greaseproof paper. To make the icing, beat the quark or cream cheese, icing sugar and honey together with 1 tablespoon of the orange juice and chill until required.
4 When the cake is cold, remove it from the tin and spread with the icing. Decorate with crystallised orange zest and cut into 12 bars. Chill until required.

Coffee Choux Buns

Preparation time: 15 minutes + 25–30 minutes baking
Makes 8–10

FOR THE CHOUX PASTRY
75 g (2¾ oz) plain flour
50 g (1¾ oz) butter
2 large Lion Quality eggs, beaten

FOR THE CRÈME PÂTISSIÈRE AND ICING
1 tablespoon instant coffee granules
200 ml (7 fl oz) milk
1 large Lion Quality egg
50 g (1¾ oz) caster sugar
2 tablespoons cornflour
150 ml (¼ pint) double cream, whipped
75 g (2¾ oz) icing sugar

1 Preheat the oven to Gas Mark 7/220°C/425°F. Sift the flour onto a plate. Melt the butter in a pan and add 150 ml (½ pint) water. Bring to the boil. Remove from the heat, add the flour and beat until lump free. Return the pan to the heat and continue beating until the mixture forms a ball. Allow to cool for 1–2 minutes.
2 Using an electric whisk beat in the eggs until the mixture is thick and glossy. Spoon 8–10 heaps onto 2 dampened baking sheets. Bake for 20–25 minutes until risen and golden. Split in half and bake for 2 more minutes, until the centres are dry. Cool on a wire rack.
3 Dissolve the coffee in 2 tablespoons hot water. Heat the milk until almost boiling. Whisk the egg, sugar and cornflour together and pour in the hot milk. Return the mixture to the rinsed-out pan with half the coffee and gently heat, stirring until the mixture boils and thickens. Pour into a bowl and cool. Fold the whipped cream into the cooled custard. Chill.
4 Mix the icing sugar with enough of the remaining coffee to make a smooth coating icing.
5 Sandwich together with crème pâtissière and drizzle with icing. Serve chilled.

Easter Bunny Biscuits

Preparation time: 10 minutes + 12–15 minutes cooking
Makes 12

100 g (3½ oz) butter
75 g (2¾ oz) caster sugar + extra for sprinkling
1 large Lion Quality egg
225 g (8 oz) plain flour
½ teaspoon mixed ground spice
½ teaspoon ground cinnamon
50 g (1¾ oz) currants + 12 currants for eyes
2 tablespoons milk
pretty ribbon, to decorate

1 Preheat the oven to Gas Mark 6/200°C/400°F. Grease two baking sheets. Cream the butter and sugar together with an electric whisk. Add the egg and whisk again.
2 Add the flour, spices and currants and mix well. Lightly knead, then roll out to a 5 mm (¼-inch) thickness. Use a bunny or other shaped cutter to press out about 12 biscuits, re-rolling the dough as necessary.
3 Arrange the biscuits on a baking tray and brush with milk. Make eyes with the extra currants and sprinkle over the remaining sugar. Bake for 12–15 minutes or until pale golden. Cool on the baking sheet for a few minutes before transferring to a wire rack to cool completely. Tie ribbons around the necks of the bunnies.

Chocolate Easter Torte

Preparation time: 15 minutes + 40–45 minutes cooking
Serves 12

100 g (3½ oz) butter, softened
100 g (3½ oz) light soft brown sugar
100 g (3½ oz) ground almonds
4 large Lion Quality eggs, separated
50 g (1¾ oz) fresh brown breadcrumbs
150 g (5½ oz) plain chocolate, melted
225 g (8 oz) marzipan
4 tablespoons apricot jam, melted
200 g (7 oz) plain chocolate
200 ml (7 fl oz) double cream
foil-wrapped mini Easter eggs to decorate

1 Grease a 23 cm (9-inch) springform cake tin. Line the base. Preheat the oven to Gas Mark 4/180°C/350°F.
2 Cream the butter and sugar until light and fluffy. Stir in the almonds, egg yolks, breadcrumbs and melted chocolate. Whisk the egg whites until stiff and fold into the mixture. Spoon into the tin and bake for 40–45 minutes. Cover the cake with a damp tea towel and leave to cool in the tin.
3 Remove the cake from the tin and place upside down on a wire rack. Roll out the marzipan and cut out a 23 cm (9-inch) circle. Cut the cake in half, brush the cut surfaces with jam, place the marzipan between and sandwich together. Brush the apricot jam all over. Melt the chocolate and cream together in a small pan, stirring until melted and smooth. Cool icing slightly.
4 Place a baking tray under the wire rack. Pour the icing all over the cake, gently shaking the wire rack to ensure the cake is completely covered. Leave to cool. Decorate with the Easter eggs.

easter

With friends and family calling by, Easter is a time for celebration – bake them something special from our selection of traditional favourites.

Cherry and Walnut Hot Cross Buns

Preparation time: 20 minutes + 40 minutes proving + 10–15 minutes baking
Makes 12

500 g packet white bread mix
2 teaspoons mixed spice
1 teaspoon ground cinnamon
3 tablespoons caster sugar
100 g (3½ oz) glacé cherries, quartered
75 g (3 oz) walnuts, chopped
200 ml (7 fl oz) milk
50 g (2 oz) butter
1 large Lion Quality egg, beaten
4 tablespoons plain flour
2 tablespoons clear honey

1 Preheat the oven to Gas Mark 7/220°C/425°F. Lightly oil two baking sheets.
2 In a large bowl, mix together the bread mix, spice, cinnamon, sugar, cherries and walnuts. Warm the milk and butter together in a small pan until it is hand hot.
3 Add the milk, butter and egg to the dry ingredients and mix well. Empty out on to a floured surface and knead for 10 minutes or until it forms a smooth elastic dough. Return to the bowl, cover with oiled polythene and leave to rise in a warm place until doubled in size – about 40 minutes.
4 Lightly knead the dough and break into twelve equal pieces and shape each into a flat round. Place well apart on the baking sheet. Mark a cross in the top of each with a knife.
5 Mix the flour with 3 tablespoons of cold water to make a smooth, runny paste. Spoon this into a small plastic bag, snip the corner of the bag and pipe a cross in the marks on top of each bun. Bake for 10–15 minutes or until golden. Remove from the oven and brush the tops with the honey.

Apricot and Pecan Simnel Cake

Preparation: 20 minutes + 1–1½ hours baking
Serves 10–12

175 g (6 oz) butter, softened
175 g (6 oz) light soft brown sugar
3 large Lion Quality eggs, beaten
225 g (8 oz) self-raising flour, sieved
1 teaspoon baking powder
100 g (3½ oz) sultanas
225 g (8 oz) no-soak apricots, chopped
zest and juice 1 orange
100 g (3½ oz) pecan nuts, chopped

TO DECORATE
675 g (1½ lb) marzipan
3 tablespoons apricot jam, sieved
50 g (1¾ oz) plain chocolate, melted

1 Preheat the oven to Gas Mark 3/170°C/320°F. Grease a 20 cm (8 inch) round, deep cake tin and line with baking parchment.
2 Place the butter, sugar, eggs, flour and baking powder in a large bowl. Whisk until smooth and glossy. Fold in the remaining ingredients and spoon into the tin. Bake for 1–1½ hours until risen and firm.
3 Use a sharp knife to split the cake in half through the middle. Roll out two thirds of the marzipan on an icing sugar–dusted surface and cut out two 20 cm (8-inch) rounds. Brush both cut surfaces of the cake with jam and sandwich together with one of the marzipan rounds.
4 Brush the top of the cake with jam and arrange the second marzipan round on top, crimp the edges. Roll the remaining marzipan into eleven balls and arrange on top of the cake, attaching with more jam.
5 Spoon the chocolate into a greaseproof paper piping bag and drizzle over the top of the cake.

Last Minute Christmas Cake

Preparation time: 15 minutes + 2–2½ hours cooking
Serves 12

675 g (1½ lb) mixed dried fruits
75 g (2¾ oz) glacé cherries, quartered
zest and juice of 1 lemon
zest and juice of 1 orange
4 tablespoons dark rum or brandy
225 g (8 oz) butter, softened
225 g (8 oz) light soft brown sugar
4 large Lion Quality eggs, beaten
225 g (8 oz) plain flour
½ teaspoon mixed ground spice
½ teaspoon ground cinnamon
50 g (1¾ oz) flaked almonds

1 Place the first four ingredients in a medium pan. Bring to the boil. Remove from the heat and stir in the rum or brandy. Cool.
2 Preheat the oven to Gas Mark 3/170°C/320°F. Grease a 20 cm (8-inch) deep round cake tin and line with baking parchment.
3 Purée one third of the fruit in a food processor. Cream the butter and sugar together with an electric whisk until soft and fluffy. Gradually add the eggs, beating well between additions. Stir in the flour and spices.
4 Stir in the fruit purée and then the almonds and fruits. Spoon into the tin and level the surface. Bake for 2–2¼ hours. Cool in the tin.

Christmas Meringue Snowmen

Preparation time: 20 minutes + 1 hour cooking
Makes 5

2 large Lion Quality egg whites
100 g (3½ oz) caster sugar
75 g (2¾ oz) milk chocolate drops
5 × 10 cm (4-inch) lengths of tartan ribbon
icing sugar, to dust

1 Preheat the oven to Gas Mark 1/140°C/275°F. Grease a large baking sheet and line with baking parchment. Whisk the egg whites until stiff peaks form. Add a third of the sugar and whisk again until the egg whites are stiff and shiny. Add the sugar in two more batches whisking in between until stiff and glossy.
3 Use a dessertspoon to place 5 round heaps of meringue, (about 6 cm/2½ inches in diameter) well apart on the baking sheet. Then use a teaspoon to place 5 smaller round heaps of meringue (about 4 cm/1½ inches in diameter) on the baking sheet – these will be the heads. Bake for about 1 hour. Cool.
4 Save 10 chocolate drops for the eyes. Melt the remainder in a small heatproof bowl over a pan of hot water.
5 Use a small paint brush to paint a blob of chocolate on top of a body and place a head on top. Next wrap the ribbon around the neck of the snowman, gluing the ends onto the snowman with chocolate. Finally glue two eyes onto each snowman and paint a chocolate smile onto each face. Dust with icing sugar.

christmas

Even if you leave it to the last minute it's always satisfying to bake a little something for the Yuletide celebrations.

Index